JUST LL . YOUR HEART FLOW

Secrets to Living a Successful Life and Keeping it Real©

© Copyright November 2014

ISBN-13: 978-1502884244

ISBN-10: 1502884240

About The Author

Sifu Edward "Jockey" Anderson

Edward Anderson was born and raised in
Plainfield, New Jersey. He is the son of a minister
and blue collar worker in a working class family.
Edward was a very gifted student at the early age of
12 years old. At this ripe young age, he learned

Martial Arts, Meditation and attained enlightenment into spirituality and the religions of the world. Continuing over the years he eventually studied with top level Master instructors. He was invited and went to study Wu Shu and Martial arts in Beijing, China at the prestigious Beijing Institute of Physical Education.

Sifu Edward eventually went on to become founder of The Asiatic Arts after School Club at the original GACC (Grant Ave. Community Center) on the West End of Plainfield, NJ, under the direction of Mayor Richard Taylor. Taylor was the first African American Mayor in Plainfield, NJ. during the late 70's, 80's. Then in the 90's, Sifu founded the Shaolin Circle Martial Arts Club and taught many from varied background.

Subsequently, over the past 25 years, Edward has trained and taught countless students in martial arts, computer technology, spiritual mentoring, and in life skills development. Sifu main employment has primarily been in top corporations. As a MCT (Microsoft Certified Trainer) and MCSE (Microsoft Certified Systems Engineer) he freely taught IT (Information Technology) to other technicians. He is one who truly believes in giving back and sharing his gifts with others.

As the scripture says.

Matthew 16:26 *King James Version (KJV)*
"For what profit a man, if he shall gain the whole world, and lose his own soul?" Or what shall a man give in exchange for his soul?

Master Sifu Ed Anderson, the writer of this book, has been a bright shining light to many. He is a great inspirational teacher and mentor. Sifu is very happy and proud of this book which will bring knowledge, wisdom, and a deeper understanding of the simple keys to living a successful life.

ACKNOWLEDGEMENTS

First, I would like to thank **Lena Figueroa-Anderson** for all her support and assistance during the writing of this book. She spent countless hours in the midnight, staying up, waking up in the wee hours of the night, but always helping me to bring all the contents together. She was always there willing to listen and encourage me to write that which was being revealed to me, oftentimes *in the middle of the night.* Whenever a sudden inspirational idea would come to me, sometimes, we would build on it, discuss it. She had found it routine to read and review my writings over an entire weekend. She never even thought about sleep. Bless you Lena, my dear. I am so grateful and I thank God for having you in my life. We make a dynamic team and we are so good for each other. My family is filled with so many wonderful people and I am truly blessed to be supported by all of my wonderful sisters. **Barbara Mitchell, Christine Clark, MaryAnn Anderson, Professor Grace Luree Anderson, and Deborah Hinds.** Remember behind every strong and powerful man is a strong and powerful woman. In my case, *a* *group* of strong, powerful women who will *never* give up on me. **Never forget that!!**

Certainly, I would like to acknowledge my talented editors, **Angela B. Thompson** and **Professor Grace L. Anderson** for all their hard work in pulling all of my thoughts and ideas out of me and stringing them together in a simple, easy- to -read and understandable manner. Together with both of them, I was able to bring forth and give birth to this most wonderful book about life that I know you will enjoy "JUST LET YOUR HEART FLOW". These two women did an incredible job of putting it back together so masterfully, and for that I am extremely grateful.

Surely not to be remised, I also had a special group of people that I am in very close and in constant contact. We love and support one another unconditionally: **Lynn Hargrave, Malika L Anderson, Paul M, Antoine Roney,** and my sons and daughters whom I love with all of my heart. The past few months these people have been in my life on a regular basis. We help motivate and stimulate each other to "keep on keeping on" at work, at home, in school, and in life. What a great support network of friends and family. They have enabled me to write and convey and illustrate to the reader the basic idea of "keeping it real," and letting the truth just flow from our hearts and minds. I also wanted to share something of value with the reader that would really make a difference in their lives and that they could pass on to the next generation. Throughout my journey, I have been blessed to have some of the smartest, sharpest teachers, mentors, managers, team members, associates and students in my life. Also while working in corporate environments, and in the arts and sciences, I have met some of the most gifted and talented people to be found anywhere on this earth. Oh God!!There are so many to name, but I will not be able to cover all of them, but I want to give a special acknowledgement to 3 very influential men who were in my life, My Father, **William Anderson Sr.**, the best man I ever met in my life. Also My beloved brother, the late, **Rev William Anderson, Jr who** gave me my foundation in spirituality, martial arts, and started training me as a young businessman. He also taught me my very first martial arts techniques in Tae Kwon Do. Also **Mr. Carl Spencer,** a very consequential man who became my spiritual advisor for many years and from whom I learned a whole new way of thinking about life, relationships and being a man. These 3 Men taught me and encouraged me to do a deeper investigation of my own spiritual beliefs, to redefine my life, and to build a solid foundation with the God of my understanding. There are so many other people in my work life over the past 35 years who have influenced me, taught me, mentored me and also learned from me. I can't remember them all, but here are some of them. Professor Andy Merritt, Lynn Hargrave, Petra Massey, Marge Moschella, Ellawese B. Mclendon, Michelle M, Kay Larsen, Mary Ann Anderson, Barbara Mitchell, Christine Clarke, Deborah Hinds, Carlton Taylor, Carla Hammond Williams, Paul M, and Sheila Elder Johnson. To all of my Kung Fu students from the early days to the present who I have taught and also mentored: Hassan, Dean, Mike, Jack, Angel, Qwaili, Emilis, Cara, Brenda, Tee, Danny, Evie, Malika, Tanya, Nyaja, Angel, Kborn, Junies, Doc, Kim, Tanya, Poopa, Georgie, Vonnie, Gene, Eleanor, Harry, Loretta, Brian, Paul, Jon and thousands of others. Also my lifelong close friends and relatives who I speak to almost daily if not weekly you all know who you are. **May The Creator Bless You All. Wishing you peace, and many blessings.**

TESTIMONIALS

~Minister Malika L. Anderson
Author, Speaker, Expert Business Coach - Real
Woman's Guide, LLC Charlotte, NC

Mr. Edward Anderson (Sifu) is one of the greatest mentors and advocates that I know. For forty years, he's been a mentor and role model to many children and adults within different communities across different nations. He's been motivating and uplifting people for years with his inspiration. Sifu has given his life to serve humanity by educating people with his long legacy of Community Activism, Advocacy of Civil and Human Rights, mentoring of urban youth on Rights of Passage, literacy, and Men's and Women's Rights. With his unique expertise on Addiction and Recovery, Preventative Gang Violence, Health Care, Healthy Babies Healthy Mothers, Food, Wellness and Nutrition and so much more to his credit; he's a source of excellence for this 21st Century's millennial generation. Having studied in the United States, China and many other countries, Edward has an extensive wealth of knowledge in arts and culture. From a personal standpoint, Edward is one of the most brutally honest men that I know with a candid no nonsense approach to life; but at the same time has a heart bigger than life! He is always willing to go the extra mile for the underdog and always showing up at life's most important moments. We call this *showing up for life* and Ed has done just that! I could write a book about him, but I will just say he is a great man who has accomplished a lot and has gained so much knowledge and wisdom to share with the world. Sifu has a significant contribution to make to society and I strongly believe that his voice needs to be heard.

~Maggie Mathews
Project Manager
Dunellen, NJ

I have literally known, Edward Anderson, all of my life; therefore, I can speak to you with authentication as to his inspiration in my personal life and in the lives of many others. Sifu Edward Anderson or (Jockey), to those who know him well, has always been a huge motivation to everyone who has been blessed to cross his path in this world, that we call LIFE. He always had an optimistic outlook on life and shared that optimism with me personally. He has and continues to lift me up in spirit constantly. Edward has encouraged me to take my gifts to the next level. Letting me know that I possess my own uniqueness when it comes to fashion and design, I am strongly considering embracing new endeavors starting my own business as a fashion & interior consultant. It only takes one person to believe in you and for me, Edward is that person. Our family is a family of many talents in particular dancing and singing. My granddaughter was blessed with the Anderson Family singing DNA. As a singer himself, he has given me advice for her, on how the music industry works, what type of people to be of cautious, as she pursues her singing career. Mia, my talented granddaughter, is 11 years old; she auditioned and was accepted into the (PAAS) school which is a Performing Arts Institute in Plainfield, NJ. Without his guidance and direction she would still be in public school, getting a mediocre education instead, she will horn in on her raw talent as a vocal artist, as well as, being introduced to international education and travel. If you are looking for someone with the ability to encourage, inspire, uplift, and motivate; Edward Anderson is the person that can make it all happen.

~Lena Figueroa-Anderson
Fashion Retail Industry, New Jersey

Master Sifu Edward Anderson has been an innovator in his community for many years. He taught, mentored and created positive uplifting programs and activities for primarily youth and then the adults. He founded a human diversity club, while still in high school for people of all religions, races and creeds to get a better cultural understanding of each other. While working at the Local 4-H Youth Development office, he worked helping to create, proposals, packages, and programs and for several programs directed towards the youth within his county, that includes 22 cities and towns. He also participated in many of the diversity and cross cultural training programs including the Global Connections program which sent supplies to international students in Mozambique, Africa. He has been a Technology Instructor teaching Microsoft Certified Systems Engineer curriculum and worked as a M.C.T. Microsoft certified trainer for over 10 years. He has taught thousands of students Martial Arts,

Technology, Life Skills and music recording production. He loves people and is always willing to lend a helping hand. It is for this reason that he wrote this book to be a guiding light for people who want to find their direction and wants to stay motivated and excited. This book will get you excited and motivated. Knowing him personally, Sifu is a kind, caring, giving and loving human being. How do I know all of this about this wonderful man, it is because I am his wife. (smile) This book is the culmination of all of his knowledge and experience presented in a simple, easy to read fashion. He will be returning to school to receive his Master's Degree in spring 2015. For nearly 35 years, he's been a mentor to so many. My hope is that you may find the keys to living a successful, happy, quality life within the pages of this book.

~Carlton Taylor. Jr., Paint Engineer
Automotive Industry, San Antonio, TX

Master Sifu Edward Anderson is a lifelong friend who has been involved in the uplifting of humanity his entire life. He has done this through his teaching martial arts, technology, mentoring, volunteering, and writing several books over the

years. A true intellectual with brilliant insight concerning humanity. I would recommend that everyone from teens read this book to adult.
Professor Grace Luree Anderson
VP Investments- Retirement Funds Fortune 500
Professor of English Studies, Westfield, NJ

Sifu Ed's book is Amazing. I couldn't stop reading this book! It's an easy read and it shows some very useful and powerful ways to create better emotional, spiritual, and physical success. It demonstrates several methods to change your way of thinking and your actions in life, so that you can enjoy peace and joy every day. Sifu Edward's solutions are not "rocket science." They are simple, yet proven methods that he's tried and now shares with the average Jo or Joanne about how they can get to know themselves. This is a must read! Go get your copy today

Orlando Moor
Sr. Counselor
Harlem, New York

Sifu Edward - I just wanted to give you a few things that come to mind when I think about all the years we've know each other. I also wanted the readers to get an idea of what kind of person you are to a lot of people. You've always been an inspiration to be the best, and do your best. Today you are known world -wide, but I remember you as a young lad in the playground, singing 1st and 2nd tenor in our singing group, and managing the restaurant your father owned. Here are a few highlights that I remember well... Growing up in the church with my grandmother, I always looked at God as stern and distant. You were the first person who I ever heard talk to God like a friend. During grace you said, and I quote "God bless the trees and God bless the forest... oh yeah and don't forget Mercury Morris "(one of the NFL's most exciting running backs at that time) everyone at the table was silent for a moment, then we all started cracking up. Next on my list is the day you taught me how to make the perfect hamburger. We were sitting at the counter in your dad's famous restaurant "Anderson's Luncheonette, and out of the blue you asked me did I want to learn how to make perfect hamburger... We must have been hungry. And you proceeded to roll the meat, and roll, and roll. You must rolled that meat 50 times before you matted it down into the most perfectly shaped burger I'd had ever seen, and when it was finished cooking...still perfect. And were talking long before frozen patties in the grocery store. Those were the good old days. During a very difficult time in my life, you showed me what true friendship is really all about. I can remember calling you for some moral support. You came by my house and sat and ministered to me for quite some time. Afterwards you didn't just say, OK I'll pray for you and leave, but you took me to the store and you went down every aisle with me shopping for my family like your own, not cutting any corners until the cart was full to the tilt. As we were in line you noticed that they were no snacks for the kids and you went back and grabbed all kinds of chips and pretzels. And again I quote you saying, "If you have kids Man, you gotta bring home potato chips home for them." That really touched my spirit and it also showed me what type of caring, loving person you are. We have been lifelong friends, our fathers were from the same county in Virginia and I am truly honored to call you "My Brother". The list could go on and on. All the work you've done in the Arts, Technology, and Community Service has been greatly appreciated. There is a man that you were the first to tell me about who said, "The secret of success is learning how to use pain and pleasure instead of having pain and pleasure use you. If you do that,

you're in control of your life, if you don't, life controls you." His name is Tony Robbins. Peace and blessings.
~*Gladys Ali*
Legal Field, Atlanta, GA

I've known Sifu Edward "Jockey" Anderson for over 45 years. He is my friend, and a wonderful person who cares about humanity. He's always giving of himself to help others, especially the youth.

~*Sheila Elder, Telecommunications Designer, Atlanta,GA*
E-Exceptional D-Determined W-Wonderful A-Achiever R-Remarkable D-Dedicated

I have known Master Sifu Edward "Jockey" Anderson for many years and had the honor of knowing his wonderful parents and his siblings, intimately. I have seen the path of excellence that Edward as we call him "Jockey" by his nickname was leading two years ago. He was always destined for success. Sifu Edward is a strong, positive role model who has a purpose and displays it well from the entire spiritual and community involvement he either created or is a part of. He has a heart as big as this world and he gives to others daily. He is a proud son, brother, father, uncle, cousin, and friend that has touched many lives to this very day through his gifts of giving and showing he cares. I would encourage everyone to read this book and to get other copies and share it with friends and family… This is your time to shine, my brother. I am so proud of you. God Bless You.

~Zaid Oneal,
Banking and IT

I have known Sifu all of my life. Sifu Edward Anderson has mentored kids for many, many years. He has always shown a concern and love for the children from the city.

When I was a young kid around 6/7 years old and then again as a teenager, I participated in many of the programs Sifu either headed or was involved in. That included The Shaolin Circle Martial Arts Training for Kids and Adults program, The Universal Technology Technical Club Training for Kids and many others.

Sifu Ed is what we call a Master Teacher.

He is a phenomenal teacher with great abilities to communicate, motivate, and uplift students from varied backgrounds. He always mentored in his resident community. Sifu has been a great inspiration in my life and the lives of others to want to do better and reach further to strive for our goals at work, home, and play. I see Sifu with great compassion and I always remember his big goofy smile. I surely recommend to all readers out there his incredible books: "JUST LET YOUR HEART FLOW" and the upcoming companion publication: "THE WORKBOOK 2.0" The book will help many as it is an inspiring life guidebook.

Thank you so much Sifu!

Kamau Ali
College Student, New York, NY

Master Sifu Ed Anderson Where can I begin? Well, let me start out by saying that he has been the most influential instructor and coach in my life. He started out as my kung fu instructor but as time passed he became much more like a big brother figure to me and many others. He has used his knowledge, skills, and training to help others improve their lives. I learned a lot about life and the world from Sifu Anderson. His commitments to family, friendship, and service to his fellow man are the things that stand out to me. He has always been a source of inspiration to many others and he has taught me to go beyond my block and to stretch my mind. This has resulted in me traveling to Africa on a cultural mission some years ago. I really appreciate his unconditional love and charity. You will find his teachings in the pages of this book.

CONTENTS

FORWARD

Behold! I tell you a mystery. We shall not all sleep, but we shall all be changed, in a moment, in the twinkling of an eye.

1 Corinthians 15:51-52a

DEDICATION

This book is dedicated to you - the reader - who is in search of something new, something different, and something that comes straight from the heart.

I wrote this book as I noticed that throughout the country, and even throughout the world, there was a great need for a life guidebook. This guidebook would lift up, motivate and simply teach life skills to everyday people. This book is that guidebook that will keep one inspired to reach their goals and find an unlimited power in purpose; the purpose for which everyone is born. That purpose defined only by God. The key is only to open our hearts and find that passion and live the best life ever.

Why This Book?

This book is written from the perspective of introducing a wisdom of life among the reality of everyday living.

This book is a treasure of the supreme wisdom of life based on years of everyday experiences, living life, and dealing with real life issues, shared experiences, overcoming challenges and finding solutions to common human problems. The knowledge contained within these pages will inspire, motivate, and expand your understanding. It is shared experiences as seen through the eyes of the writer. These are regular everyday issues that many people experience every day of their lives. While this book is meant to educate and enlighten the reader, it is not meant to be the final word on life experiences. It is just a very inspiring view of life and common solutions to problems. Hopefully, you will find some very useful simple and easy methods that will transform your life and the lives of those around you. The wisdom of life is unfolding every day around us. It is our hope that this little guide will inspire us to hold on to our faith and find solutions to life and everyday problems within our world. Hoping that we all may find some valuable information and utilize our God given innate knowledge along with self-investigation and knowledge to make our lives better. May you find hope and courage to discover some of your own solutions to life's everyday problems within this book. Enjoy the journey and may God be with you.

Peace and Blessings,

Master Sifu Edward Anderson
Plainfield, New Jersey

SECTION I:

Dealing with Yourself

Chapter 1

Opening your Mind

Lately, God has been directly speaking to me and guiding me to speak out, to uplift, to motivate, and to share. To share all that he has given to me and that which I have learned on my journey through this thing called - life. I must humbly say that we must start with "letting go" of ideas of titles, rank, corporate positions and egos; which sometimes makes us think we know everything, and no one can teach us anything at all. It has occurred to me that no one that I have met, so far knows it all. When we think that we have all the answers to life we will never be free to experience life and learning at the fullest. Furthermore, if we are to learn the true lessons that the almighty is trying to teach each and every one of us so that we can become better individuals, we have to **"let go."**

Every day, as I mature spiritually, I am learning from butterflies, birds, and especially little children, who are much "*younger*" than I, some very valuable lessons about living life.

My spiritual development has been the result of the following:

1. More than 25 years of following a path of discovery, recovery, learning, study, and an unbounded search for truth, knowledge, wisdom and experience.
2. Working on improving myself to be the best person I can be.
3. Actually trying to see the real message in a situation and not being in denial of that which is right in front of my face. As they say "the truth is as simple as the nose on your face."

After many, many, years of doing active work of recovery, discovery, and letting go of the ego mentality, you too will change as you begin to really see the divinity in others who are just as equal to yourself. You will also gain a mutual respect for other's views, beliefs, and from that, you will grow. Well, I have grown. I have been taught and have taught many others. As a result of the many people who have crossed my path, I have lived and learned, and that has been a blessing. Every day, I learn something new.

Chapter 2

Why the Need to Develop Oneself?
The preparation or development of oneself through educational and personal growth (self-cultivation) promotes a more civilized individual, community and society. An important part of personal growth, and one thing that I personally know for sure, is that it takes much dedication to become the *best you can be*. This becoming the *best you can be* encompasses the development of one's self externally, internally, mentally, socially and spiritually through your life experiences.

This book is the result of many years of living this life, making mistakes, correcting mistakes, learning from relationships, and participating in one-on-one or groups in workshops, meeting, and training classes.

These relationships included:
- Many men and women from every walk of life, irrespective of race, creed, color and economic background that you can imagine.
- Vice Presidents of large corporations
- Professional men and women

- Blue collar working men and woman
- Truck drivers
- Secretaries
- Directors
- Athletes
- Models
- Teachers
- Technicians
- Sports Management entrepreneurs
- Regular common folks

This wisdom was also gained from everyday people in various diverse communities that I have encountered during the changing seasons in my life. It is the culmination of the wisdom of my father, my mother, my brothers, my cousins, my wife, my sisters, my daughters, my aunts. Not to exclude my friends and the positive men and women that I have been blessed to have had in my life now and in the past who taught me how to treat and respect all people. This wisdom I learned at an early age in my life.

I pray that this information is useful to you and that it helps you in building your relationships with the people in your life; whether it is at work, home, or in the business world; at your church, temple, mosque, or wherever you choose as your place of worship. After all, it is all about improving your understanding of self and the relationships you will have. The relationships will be in general, in friendship, with or without intimacy, thru acquaintances, thru blood, thru purpose and even in irrefutable differences. You will have many and you will need to be the best you can be while treading them all.

CHAPTER 3

The Importance of Having
Strong Support Systems

The world is a huge place. It is full of diverse individuals who possess diverse views and opinions. Many people feel that their beliefs or their priorities are above everyone else's. Yet, there are those special individuals who really care about others and their well-being who understand the inter-dependence and diversity of us all. You would do well to keep these kinds of people in your support system, if you don't already have them in your life. These people are the positive people in your life. I call them "WINNERS. All you have to do is reach out to them and they will be there to help you in hard times - when you need a hand and are unable to make the proper decisions. There are several very important people in my life whom have enabled me to make proper decisions and to avoid some of the pitfalls that I would not have noticed. I'm so blessed to have these wonderful, smart people in my life to guide me. Then there are also unseen divine energies that emanate from our parents and ancestors, though they are not physically present in your space. I refer to these special people and divine energies as my angels.

CHAPTER 4

Having a Positive Circle of People in Your Life is A Must

Having a positive circle of people and mentors in your life is imperative. I have been blessed, learned a lot, and traveled to many places. I've met different kinds of people from all walks of life: secretaries, managers, Vice Presidents, singers and dancers. I've met educated doctors, lawyers, blue color workers, factory workers and other ordinary people. I've also spent over 25 years working around technicians and engineers in my chosen career field of IT (Information Technology). What I know is that people are placed in our lives for a reason or even a season, so it may be for a short time or for an extended period of time that you may find a person from the past or future in your life. For that reason or season, and in order to get what you need to LEARN & GROW, you must open your mouth and interact with people who will help make you successful and comfortable and confident with yourself.

Therefore, remember these three things:

(1) To move away from those people who do not promote you and are always putting you down.

(2) Get a positive group of people in your life circle who have belief, faith, and trust in you. These people will make you feel worthy and motivate you to success.

(3) Always respect people no matter what their background or educational credentials are because everyone's experience is valuable and you never know where your blessing may be coming from.

CHAPTER 5

Learn How to be Yourself

If you want to really learn how to be yourself, the first thing you have to do is to Stop Lip Synching, Faking the Funk, and wearing a mask. This world teaches us to change and put on a mask for this and for that, and how to lip synch our way through life. However, after so much mask changing we get caught up and forget who we really are.

When you're acting fake you are pretending. By doing this you don't have the opportunity to maximize your relationship with people at the highest level. You're not able to take off the mask because you are too busy pretending, and your superficial side is obvious to those who are around you. They see the FAKENESS. Your relationship with certain individuals does not capture the essence of what it should be because you cannot bare it all. You cannot be real and you can't *peel* back all of the layers of self and really be transparent. Thus you cannot really get in touch with your real self. Your real, for real – self. Accordingly, if you practice being real, you will be able to get all the juice and extract everything from life that God has destined for you out of the relationship with any person.

CHAPTER 6

Learn How to Move On from the Past and Expired Relationships

At certain times in our lives, all of us became aware of a relationship in our life that had long ago expired. You see some relationships are meant for a reason and a season. After going through painful and challenging situations sometimes a relationship cannot handle the constant pressure, discord and pain. So, keep in mind that some people are not good for you. If you stay in a relationship with them, you are going to experience pain. If the pain is too much and or the date's expired, it's going to result in an unhealthy experience or bad relationship. You've got to know when to help yourself and let go. Otherwise, you will be out of balance. In battle, you've got to know when to fight, attack, retreat and surrender. Well, in a relationship you have to know when to "hold em and know when to fold em", as my spiritual brother, Carl used to always say. You must know when to implement these actions or you are definitely going to lose the battle you are fighting. You have to understand when it was time to walk away, or not to stay too long. If it's bad for you give yourself permission to get out of a situation that is going to hurt you. Even though it sometimes seems too difficult to do. Nevertheless, you have to have the build the courage to do so. It doesn't take a great deal of confidence or smarts to do this either. Just meditate about how you want to feel and dig down deep to pull out your commitment to wanting something better for yourself and as I say, *"There is no other choice, I Just have to handle it."*

SECTION II:

Improving Your Spirit Life

CHAPTER 7
You Must Have a Mirror

Everyone who is in search of their true self and who wants to grow must have a mirror. Not just any mirror, but an honest mirror that allows you to examine yourself from the inside out, and to find out who you really are. The only thing you should ever see on the outside is the determination and confidence in your eyes to move forward; the peace from a smile on your face showing contentment in whatever state you find yourself; and your nose not turned up in allowing others to come close enough so they may impart to you what is needed. If you are seeing your skin complexion, your pretty or handsome face – you are not looking hard enough. You are definitely not looking at the image if you think you are ugly and not worthy.

Find out who you are by seeing the real you. This image should come from your dreams, your goals and your focus. You can't be happy with a frown. You can't be content with whatever life throws at you by sticking out your lips. You can't be determined if your eyes are not focused showing attention to what is a head. You can't attract folks if your face has a scowl. Practice in the mirror and let your face develop into an expression in changing the inside person to the better person moving forward on the outside. ◆

CHAPTER 8

How to deal with betrayal and overcome bitterness

This lesson was a difficult one for me to learn, but I learned it through pain, suffering, and betrayal. I learned it by being forced to let go of a lot of life problems, roadblocks, and situations.

Throughout life you are going to be betrayed, but whatever you do, don't become bitter and definitely do not become stuck. Move on and grow. Don't stay angry, resentful or negative. If you do it will sabotage your success. We all go through it where someone we love or trusted, or sometimes even a relative or family member betrays our trust. Don't let it pull you down. As we say in Tai Chi; "you must become soft as cotton, but bend and sway like a willow, never breaking or cracking."

There is a story in the Bible of Judas who betrayed Jesus. Just like Judas, unfortunately or fortunately, some people will do you harm or betray your trust. This is REAL LIFE and people may try to hurt you, to use you, to exploit you, to sell you out, to betray you and throw you under the corporate bus! The key to surviving through this all is being aware of these people and understanding how, *let me repeat this*, understanding how their actions are fueling your future. This was what happened when Jesus was with Judas. I love when he said, "Judas, do what you came to do to me, and do it quickly." Wow!! He understood that Judas was going to betray him from day one. Jesus knew that Judas was throwing him under the bus for 30 pieces of silver. Yet, Jesus did not let that get in the way of helping Judas, taking him in, loving him, teaching him and training him. Jesus was not worried because he knew at the end, he had already won. Jesus didn't spend or waste time trying to get revenge on Judas. You should learn from this lesson in the Bible that even though the ones you love betray you, God has a way unbeknownst to you of fixing things. We all know what happened to Judas in the end right? However you see it, it seems to me the betrayal of Judas was already destined to be, as God's specific assignment is destined in your life. So be mindful that God's outcome is the ultimate revenge. He is the only one that will judge us and he alone will find the right remedy. Also some people can only give you what they have or learned. Some come from a painful family or existence and the only thing they can give you are their negative karma. Whenever you are betrayed, do not worry about the betrayers as long as you are still able to complete your project and reach your goal.

CHAPTER 9

Personal Belief System and Faith

I have spent many years on the path that leads to the light. By light, I mean finding the correct direction I should take in life or life's decisions. In my search I have encountered many teachers, learned many lessons, and have gone through many experiences. One of the most important experiences I wanted to share was my search for God and what it has been like for me up to present. As part of my religious simplicity workshop, I am going to interview four people who we are going to talk about religious and spiritual beliefs and their faith in a higher power or God. We will share our research and show that ALL people can and should worship God in their own way and gain an understanding of where their faith comes from. And if, their foundation is built on love, they can't go wrong. My research and discovery began by attending various places of religion. My understanding included the basic tenets of common respectable human behavior. I came to believe in my understanding of God's peace. I studied religiosity for many years and I know how it

works; and that it made me feel uncomfortable.
Some religious leaders will tell their religious
communities (otherwise known as congregations):

*"If you don't do this, then you're going to hell, or if
you do this, then you're in God's good graces, or if
you give me a lot of money, then you're definitely
going to heaven."*

I've listened to that rhetoric all of my life! Here's
my take on it. I believe that you should know and
help more people who are struggling, homeless,
hungry, confused, and hurt rather than knowing and
helping more people who are rich and famous, who
live in big houses and eat filet mignon or lobster
whenever they want to. I ask the questions, "Why
not heal the sick and hungry?" Instead, we put the
responsibility to help others on God's shoulders to
carry. I say, "If God gave you a gift than you
should try and use it for his glory and the building
up of his earth and the people that dwell in it.
These are the common, ordinary people. That's
what I believe God would want us to do. We can
make the world better by feeding people who
cannot eat on their own. We're all human beings,
and as such, we have to share with other human
beings. Thus, we shouldn't keep all the food to

ourselves. We should spread hope, move where the spirit moves, and give whatever needed to someone who is in need.

I remember what my father and so many other wise people in my life told me as I was growing up. They said, "You can't take all of the fancy clothes, cars, houses, super fantastic corporate job, top notch friends, and money with you when you die." Now, don't get me wrong, I do believe that you should live for yourself. You should live life lavishly and large if *you* like to. I am not saying "don't enjoy you." But what I am saying, even after you take care of your wife, children, parents, and relatives, you should always save some for Elijah, or save a plate for a hungry neighbor. This bit of philosophy was shared with me through my father and mother. They were just heavenly, loving, giving, country folks who gave where it was needed, loved with all of their hearts, and put God first.

Finally, you should develop your own relationship with him, your higher being, based off of your own personal connection. The preacher, your sisters and brothers in Christ, your family, NONE of them will be there with you when you die, when it is your time to be judged, so you need to know and learn God for yourself.

Lord, I pray for all my brothers and sisters no matter what the official religion may be. I just pray that you bless them to be strong, to be righted with the abundance in their lives and their families, in the workplace and schools, in the field, and at the plant. I pray that each and every one of you sow and reap an incredible harvest. Thank you.

CHAPTER 10

Each of Us Has an Angel

Each and every one of us has a spiritual guide. Some people refer to it as an angel that guides you during your long lifespan. You can feel the presence of a spiritual force that guides you on the right path through prayer and meditation.   My spiritual advisor used to always say, "Angels are there, watching us and touching our lives." Their presence is everywhere."

SECTION III:

Improving Your Future

CHAPTER 11

A New Beginning

Goal Setting: Why do we need to make a list of what we want and how it helps and motivates us to succeed? Everyone must have a goal or a set of goals they are there trying to achieve. This is just human nature and wanting to do more, be more and see more. If you do not have a goal then you need to be motivated. So here's a simple exercise to motivate you through goal setting.

- What are your top three goals that you would like to achieve or do in the next year?
- What are your top three things that you would like to have in the next year?
- What is one of the top three places you would like to go?"

Categorize each of your top three things you would like to achieve/do, like to have, and like to go. Check on yourself each week to see what movements you have made to progress towards your goal. ◆ In setting goals it is the important to have a plan. You must have your very own master plan to success. I will do a full goal setting workshop in the next book. Part 2 of this book

I have been goal setting for many, many years. There's a picture of me in this book when I attended a college workshop at Morehouse College, in Atlanta Georgia, back in 1978. At the time, I was reading and setting goals for my future education and my life and all I had was a pencil and a piece of paper. I call this goal setting "on the go." You have to use whatever is at your disposal when random moments give you the opportunity to motivate and uplift your brain to reach whatever goal you're trying to achieve. In other words, you just sitting there, waiting for things to happen; *is not going work. Take the opportunity, no matter where you are and start to write. Make a list of the goals you want to achieve if you want to change where you are to where you want to be.* This is my goal setting "on the go" of what you can achieve when you push yourself.

Goals can give you the vision to stretch your hindsight (past) and foresight (future). Together, taking an honest look at your past and what you would like to plan for your future can help you understand and shape your insight (present) into successful goals.

Remember the following when trying to accomplish your goals:

- Have A Plan
- Courage
- Execute the plan
- Feedback
- Correct any obstacles/challenges
- Don't be so serious. Look at it as a game and make it fun. That way it becomes easier.
- Re-Execute again and again until you reach your goal
- Once you reach your goal, celebrate your own success.
- Print yourself a Congratulations Success certificate and take a picture and hang it on your wall or desk or refrigerator.

If you already practice walking into the winners circle, practice making acceptance speeches, it will help you visualize succeeding in your mind's eye.

SECTION IV:

The Master Keys That Work In Real Life

CHAPTER 12
Master Keys to a Successful Life

Self Esteem

In order to build really good friendships, one must be a friend to one's self first. Loving others is predicated on self-love. Try to build the foundation of any friendship by first taking an inventory of the gifts, joys, and strengths that you can offer to that relationship.

After so much degradation in this society where men are considered as dogs, and women are sometimes portrayed as just being a physical object, I know that it can be hard to appreciate one's own divinity. But, you must learn to love yourself first. I suggest that you take yourself out on a date. Don't be afraid to put yourself first. If you don't take care of yourself, there will not be anything left of you to take care of others. How you treat yourself will set the standard for how you want to be treated and how you will allow others to treat you.

Lastly and most importantly, do not ever forget to thank God, your higher power, for the opportunity and appreciation to be blessed with the gifts you have and the ability to love - thyself.

Having a Positive Self-Image

Embrace your features; your complexion, your curves, and your freckles. However, even if you want to re-define or sculptor yourself, you still have to love the base that you come from; that original essence, YOU. The real you! Not you with the fly outfits, the high-end cars and trucks that you drive, or the makeup, jewelry, tailored suits, and fur coats that you wear, but the REAL OLD NATURAL YOU!!! Your life now and in the future, depends on how you see yourself. Therefore, having a very positive self- image is the beginning point to getting you to self-freedom. Please, I beg of you. Whatever you do, don't go around hating yourself. I know that the TV, as I like to call it "The Stupid Box", will have you believe that you must **look** like any image seen on TV or even in a magazine that is doctored up with makeup or software painting techniques. You are not "Beyonce", a model, Jay Z or Bill Gates. There looks and talents are not yours!!! STOP trying to be someone else and be who YOU are! ♦

Remember, our features connect us to our family, our ancestors, our cultures and our civilization. You need to know that embracing yourself keeps you in touch with knowing where you came from. Your features define your heritage and identify your lineage. Knowing who you are is really what counts at the end of the day and as you move thru life.

<u>Being Beautiful: Loving Your Image</u>

Are you loving yourself and treating yourself like you are God's gift to this earth or are you treating yourself like you are beneath the animals? Let's find out. Ask yourself these questions:

1. Do I dress inappropriately? As a man do I wear my pants sagging or a woman with too much cleavage?
2. Do I behave like a snake?
3. Do I respect men or women on some real life TV shows? (I.e. women because of "Real Housewives of Atlanta", "Mistresses", men because of "The Bachelor", "Jersey Shore"…)
4. Would my grandparents, parents or favorite Auntie/Uncle be proud of how I look and act?

5. Would I want my daughter/son to grow up just like me?

6. Would I be proud of my life and be okay with it being sprawled across the front pages of the NY Times, Google, Facebook, Instagram or Twitter?

Depending on your answer to any of these questions you need to reexamine yourself and your actions and make some changes to your attitude and your life. If you cannot answer honestly than we need to have a longer conversation about self-respect.

Renewing Your Mind

Your mind can be the battlefield for all of your battles, past, present and future. You can experience battles with yourself, family, Co-workers or the person that cut you off on the road or took your parking space. Battles can occur with just about anyone. This can be your self-created, self- imposed prison. That is, if you let it. You have to free your mind and break it up, my friend. Break out of that prison. Break those shackles. Break the chains that are holding you back from becoming that man or woman you wanted to be as a child. So many people are destroyed by hearing hateful and negative words during most of their developmental years, and now it is up to you to replace those words with words like: "I am a beautiful Queen or King" and "I am strong" and "I am intelligent." "I love my shape, size and age." Choose clothing that compliments your assets, not those that put your assets on display. Choose clothing that shows your positive attributes. ♦

Start with the full and total acceptance of yourself, your body, your curves, your hair, your mind, your voice, your representation to others, and how God has created you.

I cannot express this enough that your beauty goes beyond the imperfections that you see in the mirror; such as the big bump on your nose. Beauty is the residual effect of emotional, spiritual, and physical wholeness. Look in the mirror and see the goodness of your spirit. See the emotional happiness derived from being good to *you*. Tap into that inner beauty. Let your inner beauty shine through to the surface like the glowing star that you are.

Having A Positive Mental Identity

Why is the renewing of the mind important? Have you asked yourself that question? Well, the answer is not complicated. It's simple. It's because your mind can become a battlefield. The way you see yourself becomes embedded in your mind as to who you are and worst who you limit yourself in being. Remember to look in the mirror. Do you look at yourself and say, "I look good. I am a king or a beautiful queen." Beauty must come from within. It is something that holds you together. I call it having wholeness. Beauty is a kind of spiritual wholeness, physical wholeness and balance.

At the end of this book I will let you do some homework and self-study. This will constantly refresh your memory and allow you to internalize the principles within this book.

Dealing with Self-Inflicted Pain

In changing one's self or making any progress towards change, one thing is of utmost importance and that is the realization that some pain is self-inflicted. Not only can pain be self-inflicted, but caused by our own attraction to familiar pain. Case studies will show that no matter how painful something is, even at its worst point, because we are familiar with it, we will continue to embrace it. Consequently, it can become a cycle that we can get caught up into and never know how to respond to and or correct it.

Likewise, if we allow ourselves to be afraid of change and if we are not honest about who is inflicting the pain on us - ourselves or someone we love- our pain cannot be eliminated. I know that I have listened to stories from friends and identify with those of my own. The familiar story of a person staying in a relationship and putting up with stuff that is just not good. That person may even call the relationship to be over. However this breakup occurs in a minute and yet a minute or so later – YES A MINUTE OR SO -   that same person is calling the other back. The person who called for the breakup – let us call them the victim – gave no time to heal and less time to take stock on whether totally moving on was the time necessary to heal FROM this now toxic relationship.

Unsurprisingly however, the victim realizes that nothing had changed in the short break up. It was not the thought of everything good in the relationship that called them back, but only the familiar and the sting of loneliness. The pain in the relationship was familiar and better to be with someone than to start a new with someone else. That was to unfamiliar. ♦

Change in this case is hard to just break from. It is more because the victim has not realized they have become part of the problem. The problem was that a couple sometimes may need to end because there is no longer growth in the direction of the relationship. Perhaps the problem is that the other person is abusive because of insecurity, control issues or just plain meanness. Whatever the reason, is the victim cease to be a victim. They are now self-inflicting the pain they are now experiencing. Until they realize they are part of the current problem – the problem will not be worked out so easily. Once they realize they are now helping to self-afflict pain on themselves in the relationship then they can change by truly BREAKING UP and moving on. Knowing the truth is the key to bringing upon change. Change is easy when your eyes are open to who is responsible for the problem in the relationship. It is harder when the person experiencing the problem is now responsible for keeping it going. All along the answer was there on how to move on and at anytime they could have said, "Wow, I could have had a V-8!

Paying Attention to your Diet & Health

Put the cookies, cakes, and ice cream down! I know that emotionally, it makes you feel good, but the consequences of diabetes, heart attack, high blood pressure and high cholesterol, to name a few, are diseases that can put you at risk. Do you want to die young? Find a good cookbook that helps you manage your meals. Find recipes that are healthy; low in fat and high in protein and begin cooking healthier foods and eating lots of fresh fruit and vegetables. Stay away from the red meat and indulge in fresh fish and poultry. Add seasonings to your vegetables and meals that you sautéed in olive oil and your experience will be phenomenal. Believe me it's not easy, but it is worth it. There is only one to say it, "Let go off the butter and fatty foods."

Getting Off of Your Block

Leave your block. I mean it! Go outside the front door in your neighborhood and walk past your block. In other words, "Don't be afraid to go other places and do other things." As human beings, we need to start discovering the world that we live in.

Some people, for whatever reason, never leave the state where they are born. Let me tell you about a young lady who had come from a small town to become a top designer for a company that I once worked for. We became friends and the young lady told me that in the small town where she lived for most of her life there was no one in her family who had ever moved away. Yet, she was planning to move away and go to London. I told her, "Good for you! You go girl! Go get the world and don't be afraid to try new things." I tell all my students to practice discovery techniques and that will help them to try something that they have never tried before. This practice of discovery in life helps expand one's mind and consciousness. I always make it a practice to take up a new hobby or to learn about something that I am curious about, and for most of you who know me personally, you know that I have always been curious. The concept of "Getting off of my Block" has helped me to grow in many, many ways. ◆

Wearing Professional and Sensible Clothing for the Occasion

How many of you pay above $10,000 for your wardrobe valued at $5,000? That is ridiculous. You spend more money on your clothes than your body and health. It's so funny how far some of us will go just to say that we are in fashion. You are crazy for fashion; sometimes we all are. The world has made us crazy. Men will wait hours for sneakers that cost more than a monthly car note. They have to have every sneaker that comes out. Some women will buy themselves 20, even 30 wigs. I ask the question, "Why?" Oh, so now you are looking to become that many different women? What's the point? Our clothing can be a presentation of how we feel about ourselves. It is also an expression of our style; our flavor. There are stores that specialize in a variety of sizes and shapes so that we can achieve just the right fit and the perfect look that fits us. Don't be a slave to the latest fashion – clothing, footwear or whatever. It might not be suitable for your size and shape, or for that matter, it may not be age appropriate.

Being Able to Slow Down-Take It Easy

Most people spend time racing through the day on full blast; trying to accomplish everything for everybody. Getting the job done at home, at work, or even in relationships requires that you calm your mind and find balance for all of the things that need to done. Plan your day and all the activities that have to be accomplished, but save time for you to relax and slow down.

Stop Working So Many Hours
Working too many hours can cause you to get cranky and tired. Sometimes you might find it hard to fall asleep or even to get enough sleep. Relax and close your eyes and just focus on the light. Spend at least 10 minutes being still. Have a quiet time for yourself. You will feel peacefulness and calm. It will help you deal with situations more calmly as they arrive. Reducing the number of hours you work will also help you to think more clearly and be more aware of your surroundings.

Traveling and Commuting Too Much.
One must be careful of travelling too much because it de-centers the spirit and unbalances your emotions. This means in order to travel, you must plan, organize and execute your trip. Each trip requires thinking and the use of energy to be the success that you want it to be. Therefore, I would suggest that you limit your travel so that you don't have to spend so much time on the planning and execution that goes along with it. Keep in mind that short trips also require planning, so if you want

a still mind and peace in your life, you will reduce the time you spend on the road.

Having a Spiritual Mentor
While I believe that everyone should be a member of a church, temple, or where ever they go to seek refuge and peace, I also believe that leaders, teachers, and preachers are human beings and they are imperfect. That is why I recommend, or I will just say it bluntly, "Don't put all my hope and faith in them. Put it where it should be and that is with God." You can worship God everywhere and anywhere.

Let's give our leaders a break. They are just plain men and women, who are just as ordinary as we are, but they are called to be a part of a different mission whereas they serve God in ministering and teaching others. We can't, nor should we ever, judge them in being inhumanly blameless in all things. It's not our job to judge.

Consequently, go find your peace and refuge in the fellowship at places that fills or meets your needs. Remember you to bring God with you, wherever you are, and that he has a purpose for your life. **He** is the head of your life. If you remember this, you will never be critical and judge or be disappointed in your spiritual leader when they fall short just like any other. NO man is perfect!

Having Unrealistic Expectations

You have to see people for who they are and accept them as regular human beings. Stop holding people to a standard that no one, or any of us, can fulfill; because by nature we are born imperfect. Stop holding persons in spiritual leadership positions to a standard other than man will fail and fall short. That doesn't mean they are no longer worthy of the position they hold and you cannot learn or trust them to lead. It just means that you bear witness of their imperfections too. Accept theirs as you need to accept moving from your own ills. Don't look upon them different than you would denounce your own imperfections or ills. Before you do - remember, not too long ago, you were in rehab, perhaps smoking like a champ, unemployed, on food stamps, or in a bad relationship. So Just STOP! Stop putting unrealistic expectations on people just because they hold certain positions in a faith based leadership position.

Learning to be Still when needed – Do Nothing

(For more information purchase my book on Meditation also available on Amazon.com)

Meditation or reflection is an integral part of inner development. I have been meditating since 1973. I have practiced it now for the past 35 years. Lately, I have seen it integrated into our culture, corporate board rooms, sports teams, health clubs and schools. Believe it or not, my Tai chi teacher worked at a school who was promoting meditation by allowing their students and staff to practice it during their lunchtime. I also worked at a Fortune 500 company that allowed the employees to practice Tai chi during lunchtime. The long term plan was to teach the students how to relax, relieve tension and how to learn to let things go. We certainly need more meditation classes and educational materials to relieve some of the hyperness and incredible ridiculous stress that is affecting our citizens and especially children and teens in everyday life. We have to teach meditation and relaxation methods and use it to promote well-being, and to reduce stress. By practicing the art of Meditation you will relieve stress and feel more relaxed. I am so grateful that I learned it while I was still in my early teens. I think that it should be a requirement for middle school, high school, and college students.

For more information, please get my book *"Learn The Secrets of Meditation in 24 Hours"* which is available on Amazon or contact me through my website. (www.justletyourheartflow.webs.com)

Staying Focused on Your Goal

In order to stay focused on your goals, you have to decide what needs to be done. You have to make an effort in doing things that are important. For example, practice speaking in front of the mirror or start small by practicing with your family or friends. When you speak to your audience speak clearly, look at the people and be relaxed. Talk about what is important or what can inspire people. Have a basic discussion about the weather and climate. Get involved with someone who is already a speaker who will give you points and show you how to the attention of the audience. Take notes and ask the speaker how he/she became such a good speaker!

Do Not Get Distracted by Media Entertainment. You've Got Work To Do. Forget All The "Scandals" and Get to work

Do not get distracted by television or life's dramas that pull time away from you pursuing your goal.

Time wasted for the *"Scandal" or college ball* of the week is valuable time you can spend wisely contributing to your goals. When you contribute time and energy to your own growth, it gives you the confidence and self-esteem needed to move forward. Start by reading books on different subjects; such as positive development; self-help, how to build a house, or how to meditate. Anything that will keep the passion going and keep you inspired.

Don't let anyone distract you. Too much drama in your life will bring you down, make you sad, depressed, and leave you with no energy. Pick yourself up, go with the flow, and immediately be proactive in running in the direction of your goals. Do it with a sense of urgency. Do it right now! In this society, we have too much drama going on around us. So, don't allow it to invade your home. Always keep in touch with your own FEELINGS. Stay focused. Have positive people around that you can bring into your circle. Connect with them and they will grow to be great friends.

The same energy used for drama can be used to take a college course, finish your degree or to have a part time business. Do something very positive and productive in your lives. You can be a success in any endeavor that you want. It doesn't matter what you start with, it is how you finish.

Don't let distractions sabotage your own success by stealing the valuable time that you could use to be working on yourself.

Make a list of what it is you want to obtain

For example:
- Better job
- Go back to school
- Better relationship
- Better church or temple relationship
- Self-Improvement/Development
- Better vocabulary
- Better Car
- Better House
- Better Education

Make your own list. Making a list of what it is you want to obtain will bring you closer to getting it!

<u>Try Something New</u>
Try a new flavor.
Try on new clothes at the mall
Try a new horizon.
Find a new activity.
Try a new adventure
Try a new career
Try something you have never tried before ◆

SECTION V:

Living Life on Real Terms

CHAPTER 13

Mentoring Others & Being Mentored Yourself

I learned from my own personal experiences in corporate America and from my personal relationships that male mentors are important in young people's lives. I was mentored by my father everyday from the time I was a small kid through adolescence and also as a man. My father was always around. He taught me so many things by just watching what he did in life or how he reacted to a particular experience. I was always close to him and I watched his every move; and as a result, I gained so much knowledge. I got to learn about hard work, commitment, integrity, and dedication. He taught me the importance of following through with your commitments and how dedication and determination was critical to one's success. Even though the pace seemed slow, I never gave up on anything I did. Although, at times, racism played a role in the demise of many young black men, my mentor, my father, never let me give up on anything. He fortified the importance of having a male role model in the home.

Whether you are ready or not, it is time to talk about the importance of having a male role model in a young person's life. My own personal experience, when working with people at the Kung Fu and Computer school, has shown me that it is critical to a young person to become independent, responsible, and self-confident human-beings. More importantly, young people need and must have a strong male figure to direct and guide them. For example, Dr. Martin Luther King, Jr. was an American hero. He was "no joke" and he gave his life for freedom and justice. He was that kind of man; a strong role model who was willing to pay a heavy price to change the conditions of African Americans and all people in America.

Sometimes society breaks men down and without a male role model, life can make young person weak. It can also baby the boys and not allow them to experience the hard knocks of life in order to survive or overcome issues.

There is an unwritten law of nature that says that all males must overcome bad experiences and not run away from them. They must face issues head one. I personally feel that society sometimes makes our boys and girls too soft. Society spoon feeds them and gives them the answers to challenges without having them find the answers themselves. I taught my relatives, nephews, cousins, friend's sons and neighbors that boys need discipline and need to go through tough times to strengthen their minds and bodies. Utilizing the discipline found in the martial arts, I have seen the benefits of allowing the boys to scrape their knee every now and then. We need to teach our kids to be self-sufficient and reliant upon their own means. In other words:

Be independent of outside influences, but be dependent on what influences you from the inside. Being an independent thinker will help you to become a stronger person in life.

SECTION VI:

Use Your Beautiful Gift - Your Mind

CHAPTER 14

The Need for Work & Career

Work versus Career

~*Professor Grace Anderson, New Jersey*

I grew up fully understanding what it meant to get up in the morning and to go out and punch a time clock, because my parents did this every day. My first job, though it was very low paying, was returning shopping carts for customers at the Shop-Rite supermarket located in Dunellen, NJ. This was during the late 1960's, when everyone in the neighborhood got odd jobs to help out their families. If you were a little kid, you were probably trying to raise money to buy a toy or get admission to the Saturday's matinee. I knew then that work was a way to get the things you wanted and that remained a part of my culture. It was engrained in my mind early. As a result, when I grew up, I knew if I wanted something, I had to work for it, so work was my friend.

My first real job was during high school. I worked at the Liberty Theater, at the popcorn concession stand where I served refreshments to the movie goers, making $3.00 an hour. I soon began to notice early in my working career, that I couldn't make much money in hourly jobs. This prompted me to go to college so that I could make lots of money. When I graduated from college I was on my way to making my education pay off. I got a job at a brokerage firm and worked my way up to an Assistant Vice-President. Work to me was not a chore. It was a necessity. It allowed me to travel nationally and internationally, to attend important meeting with higher level senior managers and officers of large brokerage firms. I wined and dined with all levels of people. In the workplace, I was an African-American woman that was respected and on the move in corporate America. There was never any doubt in my mind of what was the meaning of working. My work became a career for me. It allowed me to make decisions about where I lived, how I lived, where my children went to school and where we went on vacation. Work should not be an enemy; rather it should be a friend. You should let it into your life.

~*Sifu Ed Anderson - Plainfield, New Jersey*

I have been blessed to have worked in the IT Field for over 30 years for some of the top Fortune 500 companies. It has been very rewarding and I have met a lot of wonderful gifted and talented people. I have been afforded the opportunity to work in the telecommunications, entertainment, fashion, medical and other industries. In the capacity of a technician, I have been very successful in my chosen field and I have taught many others who now have careers in IT.

I could have never made it had it not been for having so many beautiful wonderful people who served as my mentors throughout my entire career. I had the opportunity to rub shoulders with some very talented and some very highly educated people, as well. Some of my coworkers at AT&T and other corporations were very famous as inventors, scientist, technicians and strategist. If I listed all the great people that I have learned from it would make up a never ending list. So to paraphrase, I will just say that I was blessed and lucky to get into IT at the right time. I worked on mainframe computers at Burroughs Corp and then Unisys. I went back to school and took over 53 technology classes to learn more about technology. I worked anywhere that I could. By remaining open minded it has really helped me to excel at my job. I felt that "…to whom much is given much is required. " So I always have tried to give back and it was, always and still is very rewarding to me to see others benefit from that which I had to share. Helping others is what it's all about, Right? So my passion is to teach and share with others to help them improve their lives. I still do that today.

CHAPTER 15

*BRING CHEER TO OTHERS AND
YOU WILL BE HAPPY
ALWAYS WEARING A SMILE*

No-one wants to be around a negative, complaining person. Always on the phone complaining about what is wrong in the world. I am not saying to ignore the problems of the world, but keep it in perspective. Try to be more positive rather than negative. ***"Ain't nobody got time for that!"***

Let your happiness be a key to your success!

Most people do not wake up in the morning wondering what their purpose in life is. For me, it just simply happened. When you least expect it, while going about your normal daily routine, that's when you discover it---your purpose in life. I never understood it until much later in my life. My purpose in life is to be a blessing to others. It is to give to others of my time, my talents, and my assets; although, my assets aren't huge!

Nonetheless, I know I have to give to others when they are in need. It doesn't matter really what it is that others are in need of, if I have it, I must give it. This I do faithfully. I give my home to those who find themselves down on their luck. I give of my time, even though I work a full time job and two part time jobs. On occasion, I volunteer on after school student projects. It's not about the pay. I do it without giving it a second thought. When someone has no money for gas or they run short of cash to pay a bill, I find it necessary to give them a hand. I have even given so much that it sometimes has hurt me. I have wondered if I will have enough to pay my own bills or will I have what I need in case of an emergency. Then, out of nowhere, I get what I need and some extra. After going through this process, time and time again, I finally realized that my job is to *be a blessing to others without the expectation of return.* I do this knowing that God will bless me and take care of me and my family. This is a major part of what I am here to do.

Life is already difficult enough, with all of its twists and turns to get confused by complicated concepts about living and giving. We all have to learn to help others and just *keep it simple*. We take things and over complicate them and then it becomes confusing. Before we know it, our lives are upside down and inside out. Then we are trying to figure it out. Which way should we go - up, down, across, sideway, backwards, left, or right? When all we really need to do is go straight through it and get to the other side.

Chapter 16

Teaching Adults and Children How to Create a Better Future

Teaching young adults and children how to create a compelling future must start with a plan. Often times, failure results because the plan is not goal oriented. A successful plan must be individually posed to reach beyond our wildest imagination, stretch deepest desires, and leave us wanting something larger than ever before.

The plan starts with creating and naming the goals that we want to achieve. The goals must be vivid as possible with clarity and detail. For instance, instead of listing that you want to achieve a higher education, be very specific and list it in this way: *I want a higher education at Rutgers University or Penn State.* Then take a step further and state what you want as your major, grade point average of 3.5-4.0, membership in a fraternity/sorority, and achieve which awards. By clearly sending a signal to your brain and to your heart, you will produce the passion that is needed to pursue these goals. ♦

Passion is a big part of goal setting, along with step-by-step management classes while they are pursuing their goals, encouragement and support.

Teach children young that if anything should go wrong or they should be halted or sabotage, dropping their goals or dropping out of school is not the way to solve obstacles.

*Remind them that successful people become successful by correcting themselves along the way even when things **DON'T** go perfect. Be sure to remind them that they have to keep on keeping on even when things get tough.*

CHAPTER 17

Just Let It Flow

When the truth comes out you don't need any planning to flow through problems and issues. It is not enough to just speak of agelessness of the spirit of God without being able to tap into that spirit. We all need to be able to access and connect to that energy source, more often. Remember, God is *wireless*. This is not just to one kind of people. This is to the working class, the homeless, the rich and famous, the ordinary, the regular ordinary ladies, guys, etc. With the best intentions of offering something positive, please know that you cannot plan the truth, *IT HAS TO COME FROM THE HEART*. Just let your heart flow and it comes out alright. None of us are perfect but we have love and concern for the people that we love and know. All we have to do is *JUST LET IT FLOW*.

In This Next Chapter Sifu Ed Anderson Speaks Openly in an Open Forum Style without any structure or planning, just honestly and openly to his audiences as he often does when he is teaching

STRAIGHT FROM THE HEART

Read This Chapter and be as natural as you can Just Let Your Heart Flow

CHAPTER 18
THE RANDOM CHAPTER
JUST LET YOUR HEART FLOW
MASTER SIFU ED SPEAKS ON SEVERAL RANDOM SUBJECTS
The Wisdom of Life and Living

REMEMBER YOUR SUCCESSES

- Remember your victories, play your own songs, play the dance competitions that you were in and placed. Reach back in your mind and feel the way you felt when you took a winning place.
- Do not get caught up in any negative memories while taking this positive inventory of yourself. Get on your own path that you want to travel on in life and just take a peek into the future and feel good about what you are about to do. Don't be afraid because in the future *you always win*. Be thankful.

- Try to focus on that which is good, count your blessings, and speak out loud and boldly. Claim your dream. The impossible dream. The one that people never expected you to accomplish.
- Take pictures of yourself or look at pictures of yourself. Yes that's you looking all clean and sharp! Tell yourself that you love - YOU…. YES YOU LOVE YOURSELF. Also accept the love from God and his mercy. Remember that he blessed you to be a child of God.
- Every time you show up just go around smiling and laughing and have a good time! How you think shows directly on your face. Never walk around with your face hanging down.
- Don't let drama or sadness pull down the beauty and/or boldness of your moments. We all have problems, but you've got to pull yourself up. People want to be around a person like you if you show them you can pull through life's tribulations. You can surely be a sign of hope to others.

You know one way to assure that you feel good is to become grateful. You see, gratitude is what makes you change your attitude from negative to positive. You can start thinking of all the simple blessings that you have in your life. Like being able to breathe in and out, being able to see, being able to taste, and smell food. WOW! Be grateful for these are real gifts. I try and become and feel grateful for the simple things. We can all be generally grateful for the big house, the gold, diamond rings, jewelry and big money. All of these things are a blessing but we should not worship them above life, family, or God.

In reality all we really need is the simple things that we have to survive. At some point, we must determine what it is we need and what it is we want. I hope that one day people become happier just having and sharing love, kindness, beauty, concern, and simple natural things.

Hold on to what is real and you can find peace. Don't fool yourself into thinking that everything that they have you must have and HAVE IT NOW! This greed has made the society constantly wanting every single thing that we see. I agree that we should all want more out of life, but we don't need every sneaker that they make, every pocketbook that comes out. Every pair of tight jeans and designer glasses that are put out at ridiculously prices way above retail. Do not trade buying these things instead of paying your rent, mortgage or other necessary obligations.

START GIVING TO OTHERS

My son likes to give away all his clothes at the end of the year to charity. He says that he is trying to simplify his life. For many years I used to give away all of the things I didn't need or that I was not using. I had two storage units I no longer remember what was being store.

There was a time I decided to give away some things that I was just holding on to. I gave away all of my ties that go back to over 50 years. Some were mine and others were given to me from my late father and brother. I just didn't have any place for suitcases full of ties. I also gave away all of my technical training books some costing over $100.00 dollars for each book. If I received any money for the books, I donated the money to the Plainfield Public Library. Man, I had so many books I couldn't even move around my bedroom. Ha ha ha (laughing).

This year I promise I am giving most of it away. There is an old saying that, "In order to get new things you must give things away." In order to prepare for the new blessings, you must let go of the old. So simplify your life by emptying old boxes of things, get rid of those bags of shoes, computers and laptops used merely for parts and stacks of books already read and reread. GIVE IT AWAY OR THROW IT AWAY!! You will feel a sense of freedom and you will not have to pay another month if they have been packed in a storage container. Think about it – it is cool to travel light in life.

When I was in high school, I was blessed with an incredible fashion sense and closets full of many, many fashionable and hip style clothes. The other thing is that I had four brothers who always loved to dress up fly in suits and long leather coats. So I had friends who may not have had as much as I had at the time. So I would just give them stuff. If they saw a coat or a suit they liked, I would say "...it's yours…here take it man… no problem." This early ability to give and be charitable positioned me to be where I am at today. I have the ability to give away stuff to help others. Especially things I am not using. Like what was I really going to do with three juicers? "Maybe my daughter or my coworker could use one. " All of my life I would watch my father donate clothes, money, transportation and housing to others. Charity is when you bless others. Even today, I still give clothes away. Man I have lost 35 lbs. and for the New Year, I am planning on giving everything I don't need away. Some of it still has price tags on it, Why? Because I never wore it - (Laughing)

LIFE IS SIMPLE - DO THE SIMPLE THINGS

The simple things - Wow! That is a very important topic that my spiritual mentor, Carl used to talk about all the time. He used to say that we as humans are ALWAYS waiting for that big bang in the sky. You know that GIANT BLESSING that makes the sky Open Up and all? He said, "Sifu, while we are anticipating its arrival, we miss the SIMPLE blessings that are all around us" god blesses us every day. Many times we let these blessings pass us by. Things like clean air and water, sunlight, and moonlight." Things like these:

1. Being Able to Breathe In and Out

2. Being Able to Smile and Laugh

3. Being Able to Feel Love

4. Being Able to Open Our Eyes Everyday

5. Being Able to feel a deep emotional connection to others.

It is about the simple things such as being able to breathe in and breathe out. Try not doing that for a moment or two to see how far that will get you. LOL. The truth is you won't go very far if you could not breath, because then you would not be standing here at all right now.

<u>BE GRATEFUL – BE THANKFUL</u>

So these simple things are a good reason to be grateful.   Just make a list of all the things that you can be grateful for. Here are just a few of mine, but you can create your very own list and hang it on your wall, or your refrigerator. I am grateful for my friends, I am grateful for my teachers, I am grateful for my students. I am grateful for my family. I am grateful for my smile. I am grateful for my loved ones. I am grateful for everyone who gets the chance to read this incredible book. I am grateful for holidays, celebrations and weddings. I am grateful to be here, in this time, in this day, still standing strong. I am grateful for all of it. I am grateful for the butterflies. I am grateful for the birds and for my pets and animals dogs, cats, and fish of the sea.   ◆

MEDITATE ON BLESSINGS OF LIFE

Now take just a few moments and close your eyes and imagine for once, that you could not see anything. Then after a few more moments open your eyes and look around you. Now that is something to be grateful for, your eyesight. Perhaps imagine not being able to hear music or to hear the sound of a loved one. Hearing is also a blessing. I love to hear the birds tweeting in the trees outside my window; especially, in the spring time.

BE BLESSED AND STAY BLESSED

Be blessed just for waking up. If you already feel blessed, then stay blessed. Sometimes people don't realize just forcing themselves to smile will change their emotional state immediately. Feeling blessed changes one emotional state in an instant.

Stay blessed and feel blessed and know that God does care about you. Know that God will fulfill your every need. Even problems can be resolved and lead your life on an incredible journey. For God is not finished with you yet. Remember that everything in your life takes place for a reason also a blessing and a lesson. Know that you are important to him. Beloved - you are not just some

"Johnny-come-lately "sitting in a pile of junk, YOU!!! Yes YOU …are God's creation. So that means that God does care about you, your family, and your relationships. God cares about your entire life. ♦

DON'T PULL YOURSELF DOWN

If you start to feel down, then immediately, pull yourself back up after being negative for a bit of time. Sometimes it may take a moment to gather yourself and get positive again. But believe me you can do it. No matter how negative you've felt over something, you can move forward to being happy again. Whatever you do, don't stay stuck in a negative state. Take your time and re-synch yourself back to success. Pull yourself back up and then start smiling, clear your mind and start feeling good again. Do this even if you have to force yourself to smile. When you force yourself to smile you trigger off the feeling of happiness within your brain and your nervous system. I always tell my students and my children to keep smiling even when the going gets tough.

MAKE FRIENDS & MEET NEW PEOPLE

Throughout my professional career, I have met many remarkable people: such as Strategist, Janitors, Managers, Barbers, Entertainers, Cooks, Scientists, Lawyers and Doctors. Even Technicians, Writers, Administrators, Tacticians, Secretaries and many, many others from all kinds of professional fields and careers.

Throughout the years of my career, I have either met or worked with all sorts of people from various fields. The one thing that I would always see in these people was the human spirit of innovation. They all wanted to "make it happen." Most of the people whom I worked with were on a quest to improve their lives. So that is what I want you to get out of this book. I want you to believe that you have what it takes to make it happen for yourself. No matter what you want to achieve, I want you to believe that you can do it. In order to be successful at work I had to believe in myself. This type of work environment made me become over excited and, having the passion that I was born with, wanting to solve every problem in the world (laughing). Sorry, folks I solved a few and I tried but I could not solve them all. (lol)

CREATE A FEELING OF WANTING TO MAKE IT HAPPEN

In order to be successful you have to WANT TO MAKE IT HAPPEN. So guess what, I went to work every day for years and years and I was able to contribute to my children, my family, and the society. By going to work every day I gained a positive feeling of acceptance.

YOU MUST BELIEVE IN YOURSELF & VISUALIZE YOURSELF ALREADY SUCCEEDING AND WINNING

If you don't think you're going to accomplish anything when you go to work or when you go to school, then you are doomed. YOU START TO THINK THAT EVERYTHING IS GOING TO TURN OUT BAD AND YOU WILL LOSE ALREADY, BEFORE YOU EVEN START.

BUT TELL YOURSELF - SORRY MR. SELF PITY. BUT I ALREADY KNOW THAT IT IS GOING TO WORK OUT SUCCESSFULLY. THEN START BELIEVING IN YOURSELF AND KEEP IT MOVING. OK?

Tell Yourself **"Dear Self, I know it is going to work out fine**. Are you ready to succeed? Then just go do it. By the way I don't like to hear that kind of negative talk. When people start to speak negatively, remove yourself from their presence. When you start thinking negatively JUST STOP IT!!! Start being positive and feed yourself positive affirmations that will empower you! Not thinking in a way that hurts you or beat you down. Start projecting a movie in your mind's eye and rehearse success. That is a real key to success.

So here is an example:

I want to go to school to be a Spanish teacher though I don't even speak Spanish fluently at the moment. I begin to walk in the direction of those speaking Spanish. Learning to listen more than I talk is my step in the right direction. Sooner or later just from visualizing and being around Spanish speaking persons, in a few weeks, I am picking up some Spanish words. I am now convinced that I have the ability to actually learn Spanish. After picking up a few words of Spanish,

I begin to use those words to speak to my Spanish-speaking friends. They interact and correct and add to my vocabulary. Guess what folks!?? Eventually over time, practice, repetition, and just from projecting an image in my mind, I begin to speak. Remember first believing that I COULD SPEAK SPANISH, and having the faith to take the necessary steps, I am now speaking Spanish more fluently. It is as easy as that! It is the same with any other skill if applied accordingly. Position yourself and move FORWARD!!!!!

CREATE A STRONG BELIEF IN YOURSELF

So you have to have an unstoppable, unshakable belief in yourself. If you don't believe in yourself than know that I believe in EVERY reader of this book. I am counting on you and praying for your success. I have faith in you that whatever it is you want to accomplish, you CAN and will ACCOMPLISH it. If you still don't believe - then go do it anyway. Act as if you believe until you really do. Keep trying and going at it and sooner or later, YOU WILL BELIEVE.

I know a lot of things I tried I had no idea in the world how I would do it - but I did. I just never stopped believing and guess what happened? What I thought I could do – I was able to do. Having a strong belief in yourself is imperative if you want to be successful.

I could tell you story upon story upon story about how I never knew what would happen along the way. I just believed that the divine connection to a higher power also played a big part in my life. Whenever things looked like they were going downhill and then all of a sudden in the changing tides of time and just fortune, they were immediately turned around.

All kinds of doors were opened that were previously closed. Opportunities that were not there for me were all of a sudden there. I'm talking about with many things: jobs, situations, connections, divine inspirations, and money. All of it was just granted to me when I needed it; and I never needed a lot. It's not like I have made millions, but I believed the minimum success was measured when I had a little more over meeting my basic needs. I just want to be happy and the people that I love to have the things that they need. I once had a good friend of mine tell me that people say they want money, but that is not what they really want, they want the things that money can buy. Would you want me to give you eight $100 bills or do you want to have a fridge full of food, gas money for work, decent clothes and sneakers that are not rundown, and money for your medical needs? Perhaps you would want to be able to help the needy or be able to lend money to a coworker, a friend, a sibling or a family member? Would you still just want the $800 dollars? No, I don't think you would. I believe that you, like me, care too much about other people, our families, our children, our parents, our friends and our neighbors. We all know that paper money is great, but it is not the end all to meeting your success and providing life's needs. Keep your faith in God and be confident that you will have what you need to meet your life's needs and "then some". You will have a peace of mind and joy in your soul. All you have to do is believe in yourself to move forward toward your goals of fulfilling your needs. Push and step by step you will gain to believe enough about yourself to JUST LET YOUR HEART FLOW.

I wouldn't take the eight hundred dollars either, because I care too much about people. I think we all do, but we get caught up in the materialistic things AND THE MONEY that make us feel like we got it going on. Only know that you can be up one day and you can be down on another day. So stay positive and know that we must still dig deep within the human spirit and find that we can overcome anything that we confront us. I believe in myself. I also believe in you. Do you believe in yourself? If you do not believe in yourself, then BELIEVE THAT I BELIEVE IN YOU. Whatever you do, be courageous and trust in God that everything is going to be alright.

Just Let Your Heart Flow

Peace and Blessings,

Sifu Edward "Jockey" Anderson

DEDICATION
THE WISDOM OF MY FATHER

There is not a day that goes by that I don't think about my father. I will see something that reminds me of him and then think back to the many, many lessons in life that he taught me which span over 40 years. My father made his transition when I turned 47 years old. But not before we could take one last big family trip to his beloved birthplace of Esmont Virginia. It is located near Charlottesville and Scottsville, Virginia. It's a full, luscious, colorful, beautiful country land. It is nestled at the foothills of the Blue Ridge Mountains, which cross several states including: Virginia, North Carolina, and Kentucky. It is so beautiful there! Some call it God's country. This is where my father is from.

Finally, I get to write about my father in this book. My thoughts become the words of how important my father was and is to me. Memories of my father flow through my mind just like a smooth flowing river to the ocean. He left such a great testimony of life, knowledge, wisdom and giving that lives on in me as a man, in my family and hundreds of neighbors, where we lived in Plainfield, New Jersey. He was a great father, incredible grandfather, and a wonderful husband to my mother of over 56 years. He was a friend to so many people who loved and looked up to him. He provided the community with food, clothing, shelter, credit, and transportation. He was a renaissance man before his time. He was born and raised in a small town in Virginia and when he went back home to visit during special occasions, the whole town knew he was there. Aunt Eula Gray tells the story of how whenever he would come to town, they would start preparing and cooking for him and she used to ask grandma, Maggie Anderson, "Who is coming here? Is it the King of England?

Mother Maggie Anderson, my grandmother, would make a fuss about him. My father had this charismatic smile and the smoothest black skin with one shiny gold frame around one of his front teeth. When he smiled, you could see it. He was a tall, thin, and very handsome man in his youth and as he aged gracefully to 86 years old. Men and women loved to talk with him in passing because he was so friendly. He made them feel important and he always respected them even when they were down on their luck. Everyone in our community knew and liked him. In a lot of ways, he reminds me of a black president, because he helped and worked on behalf of his people - his fellow man. He treated everyone with respect no matter what their race or color. He believed in equality and taught all ten of his children the same values. My father, William Stewart Anderson, came to New Jersey when he was 21 years. Before that his final stop in New Jersey, though, he worked at the big

train station in Washington, DC known as Union
Station. He told me so many stories about his life,
his adventures, his businesses, and his travels as a
young man. When you listened to him you would
become enthralled and immediately recognized his
stories to be parables, not just stories because there
was always a message and lesson for you in all of
them. This man was my biological father from day
one, but he was a father to many children that my
mother adopted or fostered in the community and
some from out of town and out of state. There
were children who had no fathers of their own,
born of single mothers because their fathers had
just left them. Years later, my brothers and sisters
still heard stories from older people who knew him
over 40 years ago. They called me from all over
the country and shared fond memories of my father
and how he helped them or their family pay rent,
mortgages, buy food, or find a job. You see my
father worked three (3) jobs. He had his own
restaurant at one time or another during the 1960's
and his own corner store in the 1970's. My father
provided goods and services for the community,
and many times he gave store credit and never
asked for it from those who could not pay. Many

times, folks could never repay their debts because of the poverty that affected everyone back then before the specials programs came to our communities to assist the poor with buying food and finding shelter.

My father helped me to experience many long and short trips. I call these trips my travels in life. I consider these trips even better than getting on a plane or train to learn about life. When my father shared with me how he, all of his adult life, drove the senior citizens in our neighborhood to the grocery store that showed me how committed he was to helping his community. I guess that is where I get my desire to help others from all walks of life, children and adults. I think, therefore, one of the greatest inheritances that I got from him was just that--his helpfulness. I will tell you that I can clearly remember him taking me to work with him. At that time, in early 1960's, imagine my father was tearing down houses as a side job. Hard work and little money had my father realized it would be more affordable to have his own construction and demolition business. He not only tore down homes for realtors that were inhabitable, but also provided space for new or rebuilt homes too. He was so strong. It seemed to me that he could tear down a house with his bare hands. He would recruit and hire people from the community to help him with his work and he would pay everybody fairly, even if he did not get paid. That didn't always go over well with my mother. (smile) Soon, his small actions and his hard work paid off. He started Anderson's Construction Company. Even though he didn't earn a great deal of money, he would get large chunks of money at various times that would allow us to buy a new family car or allow my parents to fill the cupboards and refrigerators with lots of food and even help countless other families. But sometimes it took a very long time to **get paid** for his jobs. His small company helped a lot of people in the community to be able to earn a living for themselves. He was such an incredible, reputable person that when he opened his restaurant at the corner store, the people in the neighborhood trusted him and bought his products.

My brother Billy Anderson watched closely as our father made business moves that were unique to black men in our neighborhood at that time. We were making business deals with wholesalers back in the 50's and 60's when most of our communities were buying products retail. While he did demolition work during the day, our mother prepared and served food in our family luncheonette which was located in the west end of town for almost 30 years. It was called Anderson's Luncheonette. Those were the good times for our family. And entrepreneurial spirit lives within me today. The store that my father had in the 1960s was located on West 3rd Street across from the Elks Lodge. I can remember when I was 4 or 5 years old and went to work with him. He let me get behind the counter and I used to always want to count the money. When I became 6, he would take me to the construction sites and let me clean off the bricks that came from the demolition of the houses he tore down. I remember clearly, he paid me and my friend, Skitchy, 5 cents for each brick we could clean off. Man we cleaned those bricks so fast it was amazing. He tore down houses between running a restaurant, and also working the 3rd shift at a boot manufacturing company in South Plainfield called The Tingley Rubber Company, from which he retired at age 65. But though he retired from Tingley, he joined my mother in volunteering. They volunteered and maintained the

Plainfield Seniors Vegetable and Fruit Garden located on West 2nd Street and Liberty Street, right next to the Projects (Elm West Gardens). Not one to sit still, he also began selling Fresh Organic Vegetables to the community from his Van and Station wagon which was parked near the garden or near Judkins on West 4th Street and New Street. He sold his products to the community when he wasn't giving them away. Subsequently there came a time even my wife, Lena and I would work with my father and my mother sell vegetables and fruits. Lena was very close to my mom and dad and she used to work in the garden and get up with my mother at 5 AM and go to the garden to work and do hard garden work. That's when I knew she would be the one for me. Because any woman who can get up before the Sunlight at 5 AM and go and work in a large humongous vegetable garden digging ditches with your mom is the one for the job. (lol). My mother was so wise. She offered Lena to work with her in garden to see what "she was made out of. I know now and anyone who knows Lena knows that she had passed all of my mother's tests. When my mother was alive - before she made her transition in 2002 - Lena and her were best friends and she shared some of her cherished recipes, like Carolina Sweet Potato Pies, Bean Pies, Macaroni and Cheese. Mom made it so that Lena could carry the tradition forward and surely satisfy me – her baby boy. HA HA Now - if you ever had the chance to work in or at a garden or to load and unload vegetables, especially melons all day, then you would know how much mental and physical energy it takes to do this. This type of work is very, very demanding and requires a lot of discipline, mental, and physical energy. After working in the garden and selling vegetables on weekends with my father I figured something out. After all of those years of Training in Kung Fu and Martial Arts and even training in China with the best of the best trying to develop a high level of Internal energy, a light went off in my head. This is when I recognized that my father had such an enormous amount of Mental and Physical Chi Energy that was passed down to me through his DNA coding. I recently received the DNA Code tracing of my family from my cousin in Virginia. My cousin did an extensive research from Africa – the Mother land – and continue to feed me historical updates. I have it right next to me as I write. My father's Chi was enormous and my mother's Spiritual Chi Energy was also enormous. Both of their sides of the family have enormous (Internal Spiritual Energy) and it was in there DNA that was passed directly to me. I am a direct descendent and the last living male child of my Mom and Dad. It was no wonder I grew up with the ability to juggle many different jobs simultaneously. He was an independent black man with three businesses so that he could provide food and clothing for his family, his children, their children and generations to come. I love and miss my father sometimes day after day after day. On some days I remember the two days before he left us. I was in the hospital room, just him and I, and I asked him "What am I going to do without you here with me to guide me, Father", and he smiled and answered, "Don't you worry my dear son, I will never leave you. Whenever you need me, just look right over your shoulder and I will be right there." It is at those times that I realize what he was trying to tell me is that there is a spiritual world that cannot be seen, but it is still real. He told me then that he had a dream of my late brother Ronnie and my mother before he made his transition within 24 hours later. My father provided shelter for five boys and five girls, their children, their children's children and generations and generations of friends, relatives and adoptive children who now live all over the world and work across many disciplines. I am so grateful to have had him as my personal mentor and my Father for 48 years. **I Love You So Much Father**. I promise to continue your legacy of unconditional love, giving, forgiveness, concern for my fellow man and woman. God Bless you Forever, Father. I feel the light shining down on me. Yes and I see you looking right over my shoulder.

The Immortal William "Bill" Anderson, Sr. My Father, Yes. The Most incredible man I ever met *Just Let Your Heart Flow*

Your Loving Son,
Sifu Edward "Jockey" Anderson

Sifu's Prayer For The People

A Prayer of Peace and Comfort for All People of Various Faiths Written by my cousin: Ms. Holly Rhea

I wrote this prayer at the request of my beloved cousin, Sifu Ed Anderson. Although I wrote it for him, he insisted that we share it with a wider audience in his monumental book "JUST LET YOUR HEART FLOW" This is a prayer that helps me get through the day. You know prayer is not quoting scriptures, it is an intimate conversation you have with the Father. It is not just when something good happens and you want to thank him. Praise his holy name and give thanks in all. To my brothers and sisters when you need to lean on someone, turn to the father and take it to him in prayer.

When I think about all the goodness the Lord has given me I just want to thank him. So here is a prayer for all of you.

Father, I come to you with a humble heart. I thank you for each and every sunrise and sunset you have given to me. I thank you for all that I have been through. Even in the turmoil and strife I thank you. I know that sometimes I have to go through some things to be prepared for what is about to take place in life. Even in the midst of my storm I thank you. When I think about how you love me so much that you died for me; so that I can live for you. I just want to shout and say thank you. Lord there is nothing that I can't do without your grace and mercy. When I fall you lift me up. I know that all things are possible in you; who strengthen me. Every day of my life, I thank you. I thank you for the healing of my heart when broken. I thank you for making a way out of no way. I thank you healing my broken body. Lord you know my struggles, trials and the tribulations. I go through and you know my heart. Lord, I thank you for the strength and courage. I thank you for the peace and comfort that you have given me. Lord, I thank you for the laughter and the joy as well as the sorrow. I have so much to be thankful for. Lord thank you so much for loving me your child. Everything I have is because of you. Oh thank you Jesus, in your name, I pray and say

AMEN!

The Keys To A Successful Relationship

Keep Loving Each other

Keep Having Faith

Keep being patient with each other

Never Give Up

Never Lose Hope

Always Apologize When Necessary

Never Stop Dreaming

Always Look for The Good in Others

Always Lift Each Other Up

Always Be Positive with Each other.

Always Keep People out of your business

How to Be Fantastic

(Sifu's Quick & Easy Method)

1. Create a New Exciting You

2. Concentrate on Improving Yourself

3. Speak more directly and clearly to people

4. Make a New Set of Exciting Goals

5. Start Behaving like you are a Head of State

6. Walk and Talk Like this is your Father's house.

7. Being Nice but know that you are # 1

8. Start using words when speaking to others that fit the new you. Use words like: Fantastic, Incredible, Spectacular and phenomenal when people ask you how are you doing or how do you feel.

To get a more intensive Fantastic List go to the website: www.sifuslifelessons.webs.com

Start a Basic Workout Plan

1. Start Walking and moving around
2. Start Stretching and getting flexible
3. Start building your muscles up
4. Start performing some basic calisthenics
5. Create an area of the home where you can go exercise and use that area everyday
6. Try some basic exercises to limber you up at least 3 times a week
7. Start doing something as soon as you are cleared from your doctors.

Sifu's Ed Picture Gallery

These are photographs of some of the very special people in my life. These people motivate and encourage me in my life and are a part of my world. There are many others, but I could not fit them all in this book. There is a more extensive collection of photographs that we are cataloging on our website. It is a work in progress. I believe that you should always have photographs of your loved ones near you. I keep them next to my computer, on my desk at work and also in my wallet. For some reason it makes me feel closer to them and as if they are with me especially my ancestors who have made their transition.

Sifu Ed Anderson

William & Rev Grace Anderson
Sifu's Parents

Mother, Rev. Grace Anderson
receiving her Master's Degree

**My Father, William S Anderson, Sr.
and I at a family gathering.**

My wife Lena and Sifu on a cruise to a beautiful Island

Sifu singing in a talent show with Sonny & The Softhearts. A Legendary Singing group from Plainfield, New Jersey back in the 70's Swedish Knits, dark shades, and wide brim hats.

The Seventies

Sifu at PHS. This is how we used to do it. Dress Button Down Shirts, Swedish Knits, Trench Coats, Dark Shades, Hard Bottom Shoes

Sifu at The Entrance to Legendary Shaolin Temple in China

1985

My Late Beloved Brother, Rev William Anderson, Jr. aka Billy, A natural born leader and mentor

Sifu Chilling in The Park

Central Park, New York City

Sifu's Danny(son), Evie(daughter) and their Mom (wife))

Sifu says Teaching is my Passion

Sifu's friend and Kung Fu Student Jack S. A Championship Martial Artist and an Incredible Attorney

Sifu Teaching a Seminar for Youth at Our Story Bookstore, 2001

Sifu with beloved daughter Dyshera and wife Lena Anderson

In Washington D.C

(Drunken Style with my friend Ken G

Lena and Daughter Evie

Order More Copies.

Got to: <u>www.amazon.com</u> or

To contact Sifu Ed at

email:Edward.anderson7@outlook.com

email2: <u>Edward.eanderson@gmail.com</u>

Available for Speaking Engagements,

Book signings, Club Presentations

Universities, High Schools, Charter

Schools, Churches, Temples, Mosques.

Sifu Edward "Jockey Anderson

Keynote Speaker & Workshops

Available for:

Speaking Engagements,

Book signings,

Club Presentations

Universities,
High Schools,
Charter Schools,
Churches,
Temples,
Mosques
Graduations
Anniversaries

"Just Let Your Heart Flow" is keeping you connected with it's just released companion workbook
NOW AVAILABLE at Amazon.com !!!!!!!

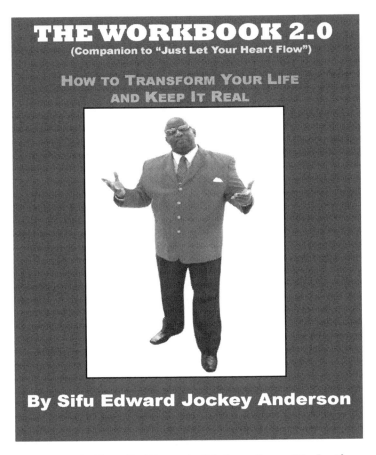

Order A Book For A Friend or Relative
Order Directly from Amazon.com website
ORDER 10 BOOKS FOR GROUPS

Order Additional books For A Friend or Relative
Order Directly from Amazon website

Coming Soon:

Meditation Learn The Secrets To Meditation within 24 Hours

Self Study

_____

_____

_____

_____

_____

_____

_____

_____

_____

_____

_____

_____

_____

Self Study

Self Study

Self Study

Notes

Notes

Goal Setting Workshop 1

Goal Setting Workshop 2

_____

_____

_____

_____

_____

_____

_____

_____

_____

_____

_____

_____

_____

What Are Your Dreams?

_____

_____

_____

_____

_____

_____

_____

_____

_____

_____

_____

_____

What Are Your Dreams?

THE END

35283488R00090

Made in the USA
San Bernardino, CA
20 June 2016